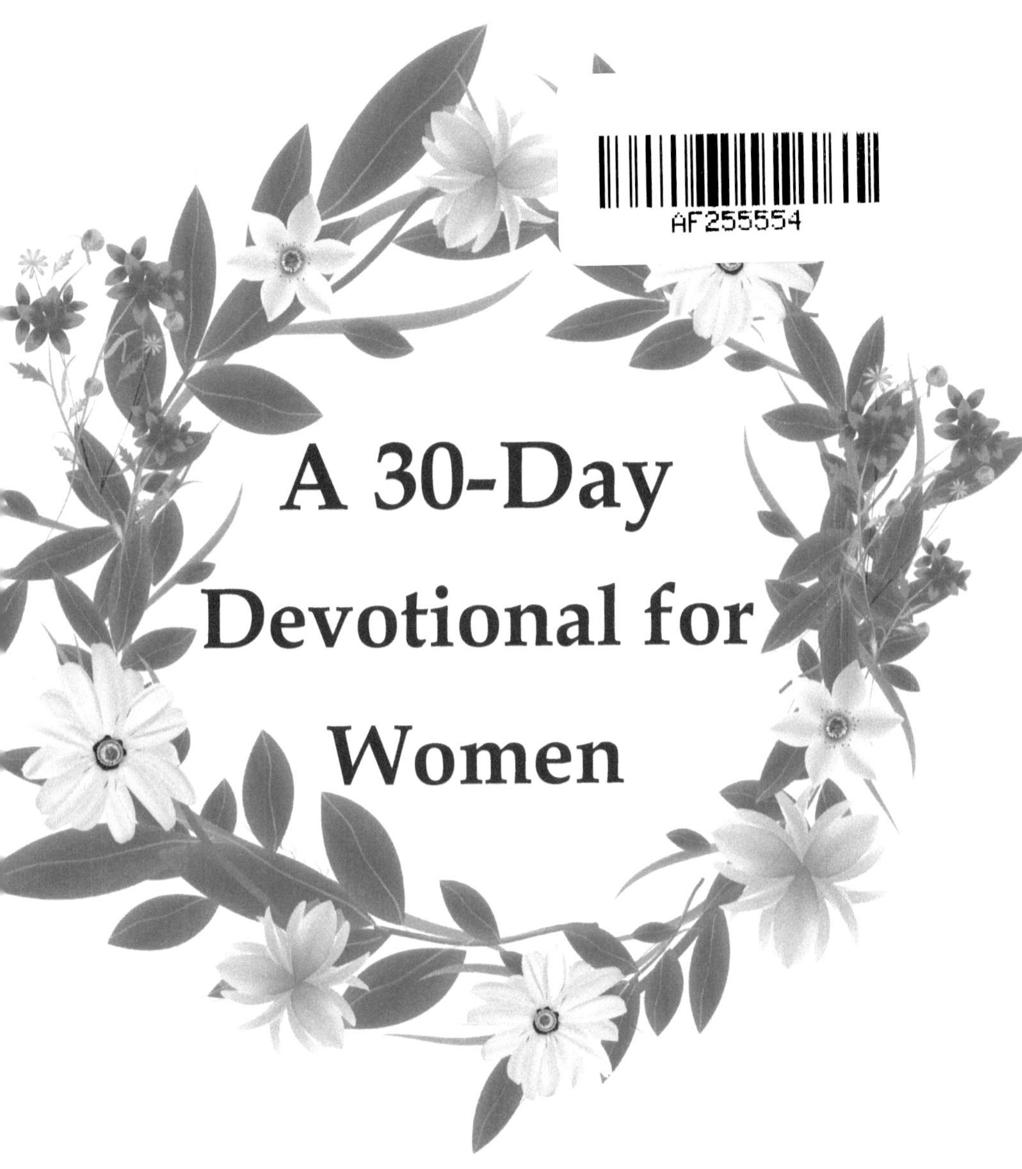

A 30-Day Devotional for Women

Connect Deeper With God To Move From Anxiety and Fear To Faith, Strength, Love, and Lasting Peace In Just 10 Minutes Per Day

ROBIN KITE

"May God's grace help you fix your eyes on His unchanging character, reminding you that peace is found not in changing circumstances, but in His steady presence."

-Robin Kite

Unless otherwise indicated, all biblical citations were taken from the *New Living Translation* of the Holy Bible.

TABLE OF CONTENTS

BONUS #1

The Peace Plan

■ Your Free Gift

As a way of saying **thank you** for your purchase, I'm offering **The Peace Plan** — a simple, powerful framework to help you reset your mind and heart in moments of anxiety or overwhelm.

■ Get instant access here:

■ Scan the QR code below to download your free Peace Plan card instantly:

Made with Flodesk

■ The Peace Plan Framework

Pause – Take a breath. Step back from distractions. Give yourself permission to slow down.

Pray – Whisper a short prayer: "Lord, bring me clarity, comfort, and strength."

Promise – Speak a Scripture of truth over your heart. God's Word steadies you when life feels shaky.

Plan – Choose one small, healthy step you can take today to move forward in faith instead of fear.

Peace – Rest in God's unchanging character and let His presence anchor you.

■ Example Peace Plan in Action

Pause: Close your eyes and take three deep breaths.

Pray: "Lord, steady my thoughts and remind me You are near."

Promise: "You will keep in perfect peace those whose minds are steadfast, because they trust in You." — Isaiah 26:3

Plan: Write down one person you can encourage today.

Peace: End with gratitude, thanking God for His constant care.

■ Tip: Print this page or keep it handy in your journal so you can use it whenever you need a reset.

How to Use This Devotional

This devotional is designed to walk with you through whatever season you find yourself in. You may use it for quiet personal reflection, journal your way through the daily prompts, or share the journey with a friend. Each day is an invitation to pause, breathe, and turn your focus toward God's faithful nature, rather than the constant changes of life.

1. Begin with Prayer

Settle your heart before God. Ask Him to open your mind to His truth, surround you with His comfort, and give you courage to remain focused on Him. Prayer prepares your spirit to receive His peace and steadies your thoughts as you begin.

2. Read and Reflect

Take your time with the Scripture and devotional. Read slowly, allowing the words to sink in and rest in your heart. Notice what stirs within you: a promise, a reminder of His faithfulness, or a word of hope. Use the daily reflection to record what stood out to you and how God is speaking to your heart. Over time, you will begin to see patterns of His guidance and care in your life.

3. Carry One Truth

Choose one truth from your reading to carry with you throughout the day. It may be a verse, a phrase, or a reminder of who God is. Write it down, repeat it in moments of distraction, or share it with someone you love. Carrying His truth helps draw your focus back to Him when worries or fears try to take over.

4. End with Gratitude

Close your day with a grateful heart. Pause to recognise where you experienced God's presence, even in the smallest ways. Gratitude lifts your eyes above the noise of life and helps you see His steady goodness, reminding you that He has been with you through every moment.

5. Review Each Week

At the end of each week, take a few moments to look back. Ask yourself: Where did my focus drift? What truth about God steadied me? How did His faithful presence show up in my daily life? Then, choose one step to carry into the next week that will help you keep your eyes fixed more firmly on Him.

6. Remember the Journey

Learning to focus takes practice. Some days may bring peace and clarity, while others may feel like small, hard-won steps forward. Both are valuable to God. What matters most is that you continue turning your gaze back to Him. You are not walking this road alone. God is with you every step: steady, faithful, and unchanging.

"And the peace of God, which transcends all understanding, will guard your hearts and your minds in Christ Jesus." **(Philippians 4:7)**

A Letter to You

Dear Friend,

I'm so glad you're here. Opening a devotional like this takes courage, because it means you're longing for something more than what your current circumstances are offering.

Maybe you're weary from carrying too much. Maybe your heart feels unsettled by all that seems uncertain. Or perhaps you're simply longing to draw closer to God in the middle of your everyday life.

However you've come to this place, I believe you're here on purpose.

This journey is about focus. It's about learning to shift our eyes away from the noise, the fear, and the constant changes around us, and instead fix them on the One who never changes. Life may sway and bend, but God's character is steady. He is faithful, good, strong, and near. When we anchor our hearts to Him, we discover a peace that circumstances cannot shake.

Over the next 30 days, we'll walk together through simple yet powerful reminders of who God is. You don't need to be perfect or have it all figured out. You don't even need to feel strong to begin. All you need is the willingness to lift your eyes and take one small step each day toward focusing on Him.

My prayer is that as you lean in, you'll find a new steadiness rising within you, not because life suddenly becomes easier, but because your heart is learning to rest in the unchanging love of God.

So, welcome to this journey. I'm honored to walk beside you, and I can't wait to see how God meets you in these pages.

With love,

Robin

Day 1

The Starting Place

Scripture:

"Let us fix our eyes on Jesus, the author and perfecter of our faith..."
Hebrews 12:2a

Devotion:

When life feels shaky and uncertain, where do your eyes naturally turn? For many of us, our gaze drifts to the noise of the world: the stack of unpaid bills, the unsettling medical report, the fractured relationship, or the long nights when rest won't come. We desperately want peace, yet we continue to stare at the storm.

But what if peace doesn't start with the storm calming down? What if true peace begins when we choose where to look?

To fix our eyes on Jesus is to intentionally shift our perspective, from what is temporary to what is eternal, from what is fragile to what is unshakeable. When we focus on His kindness, faithfulness, and unfailing love, we discover a steady place for our hearts to rest. Jesus becomes the lens through which every other part of life comes into focus.

You may not be able to change your circumstances, but you can choose where your thoughts settle. Lift your eyes. Look up, not as an escape from reality, but as an anchor in a more profound truth: the presence of Christ.

Prayer:

Lord, You know how quickly the storms around me swallow my attention. Today, help me lift my gaze to You, the steady anchor of my soul. Teach me to see Your faithfulness instead of my fears, and let Your presence quiet the chaos within me. Amen.

Reflection:

What situations have been stealing your focus? Write them down honestly, and then turn your eyes toward one unchanging truth about God. How does this shift steady your heart today?

Day 2

A God Who Does Not Change

Scripture:

"I, the Lord, do not change." **Malachi 3:6a**

Devotion:

One of the most complex parts of living with anxiety is the sense that nothing stays the same for long. What felt firm and reliable yesterday suddenly feels shaky today. The world seems to keep shifting under your feet. Yet, in the midst of all this instability, one truth remains steadfast: God does not change.

He does not wake up in a different mood. He never breaks His promises. Your struggles don't catch Him off guard, and your pain does not leave Him unsure of what to do. The same God who was faithful yesterday is faithful today, and He will be faithful tomorrow.

God's unchanging nature is not just a doctrine to study; it is a lifeline to cling to. When the headlines are heavy, when your emotions swing wildly, and when your circumstances seem out of control, you can anchor yourself in the certainty that God is constant.

He is still merciful. Still kind. Still powerful. Still with you.

Prayer:

Father, thank You that in a world that shifts and shakes, You remain steady. Remind me that I can lean on Your unchanging character when everything around me feels uncertain. Teach me to rest in the truth that You will never fail me or forsake me. Amen.

Reflection:

Where in your life do you long for stability right now? Reflect on how God's unchanging character brings you the firm foundation your heart is searching for.

Day 3

He Is Always Good

Scripture:

"Give thanks to the Lord, for he is good; his love endures forever." **Psalm 107:1**

Devotion:

When life feels painful, confusing, or even unfair, the enemy is quick to plant seeds of doubt in our hearts: "If God really loves you, why would He let this happen? Maybe He's holding out on you."

But here is the truth we must anchor ourselves to: **God is good. Always**. His goodness is not fragile, shifting with your circumstances or dependent on your emotions. It is a part of His very nature. Even when storms rage, even when prayers feel unanswered, even when your heart aches with questions, His goodness stands unshaken.

God's goodness is not always revealed in the way we expect it to be. Sometimes it comes wrapped in protection we didn't notice, lessons that grow us, or strength that sustains us when nothing else can. Other times, His goodness shows up in the small and quiet ways, a timely word from a friend, the beauty of creation, or the peace that gently fills your heart when you pray.

To focus on His goodness does not mean ignoring your pain or pretending your struggles aren't real. It means looking through the pain and remembering: His heart toward you is tender, His motives are pure, and His plan carries eternal purpose, even when today's path feels unclear.

The cross is our ultimate proof that God is good. If He did not withhold His own Son but gave Him up for us all (Romans 8:32), then we can trust that He will continue to be good in every season of our lives.

Prayer:

Dear Lord,

Good and gracious God, thank You for being my steady source of goodness. When doubts creep in, remind me of the countless ways You've carried me before. Open my eyes to see Your fingerprints of kindness around me today, both in the big moments and the quiet ones. Anchor my heart in the truth that You are always good. Amen.

Reflection:

Where have you recently struggled to believe in God's goodness? Take time to ask Him to bring to mind a season when His hand was clearly at work in your life. Write it down and keep it close, so that on the hard days you have a testimony of His goodness to remind your heart.

Day 4

He Is Always Faithful

Scripture:

"Your faithfulness continues through all generations..." **Psalm 119:90**

Devotion:

Faithfulness is not simply something God does—it is who He is. His character is steady, unwavering, and true. To say God is faithful means He is entirely trustworthy, perfectly reliable, and absolutely consistent. Every promise He makes is sure, every word He speaks stands firm, and every plan He begins He carries to completion.

We often measure faithfulness by human standards, but people can forget, disappoint, or even abandon us. Life itself can feel uncertain; dreams shift, relationships strain, and circumstances change without warning. If we are not careful, we may begin to project those same inconsistencies onto God. But Scripture reminds us: He never changes His mind. He never breaks His word. He never walks away from His children.

God's faithfulness stretches beyond time. What He was for Abraham, Moses, Ruth, and David, He still is today. Just as He sustained past generations, He remains faithful in your story right now. His faithfulness has no expiration date.

So when you feel unseen or forgotten, when burdens feel too

heavy to carry, let this truth settle deep in your heart: **God is still present. He is still keeping watch. He is still holding you.** Even in the silence, He is working behind the scenes for your good.

Prayer:

Lord, thank You for being a God whose faithfulness never falters. When my heart wavers, anchor me in Your unchanging promises. Help me remember the many times You have carried me before, and give me confidence that You are holding me now. Teach me to rest securely in Your Word, trusting that You never forget, You never fail, and You will never let me go. Amen.

Reflection:

Where do you most need to be reminded of God's faithfulness today? Take a moment to write down a past experience where He came through for you, whether in a significant breakthrough or a quiet provision. Let that memory strengthen your faith for the present.

Day 5

He Is Always With You

Scripture:

"Do not be afraid… for the Lord your God goes with you; he will never leave you nor forsake you.» **Deuteronomy 31:6b**

Devotion:

Anxiety is a loud liar. It insists, "You're on your own. No one understands. No one sees. Even God has stepped back."

But the truth of Scripture speaks louder: **you are never alone.**

From the very beginning, God has desired to dwell with His people. His presence isn't confined to a church building or a mountaintop encounter. He walks into hospital rooms, lecture halls, busy offices, and quiet kitchens. He sits with you through restless nights and heavy days. He doesn't wait for you to "get it together" before showing up; He meets you right in the middle of the chaos.

And here is the unshakeable reality: even when your emotions fail to recognise Him, He is near. His presence is not dependent on your feelings but on His promise.

Prayer:

Father, thank You that I never walk through life abandoned. When loneliness or fear tells me otherwise, anchor my heart in Your truth. Open my eyes to recognise Your nearness, and help me to rest in the assurance that You will never leave me. Amen.

Reflection:

Think of a time when you felt most alone. Pause, invite God into that memory, and ask Him to reveal where He was present in that moment.

Day 6

His Peace Is Real and Available

Scripture:

"You will keep in perfect peace those whose minds are steadfast, because they trust in you." **Isaiah 26:3**

Devotion:

Peace is not the absence of storms, but the assurance of God's presence within them. The world can offer momentary relief through entertainment, busyness, or distractions. Still, these are only temporary bandages that eventually wear off. God's peace is different. It doesn't deny the chaos around you; it steadies your soul in the middle of it.

This peace is not manufactured by pretending all is well. It flows when your heart is anchored in the One who truly is well, unshaken, unchanging, and faithful. The more you shift your gaze from the uncertainty of life to the certainty of God's character, the more panic begins to loosen its grip. Peace doesn't always arrive in one dramatic sweep; it often settles in gradually, choice by choice, thought by thought.

Prayer:

Prince of Peace, still the restless places in me today. When fear rises, remind me of Your nearness. When my thoughts race, redirect them to Your promises. Teach me to trust that Your presence is stronger than my worries and greater than my circumstances. Anchor my mind in You, and let Your calm guard my heart. Amen.

Reflection:

What thoughts, worries, or "what ifs" have been robbing your peace lately? Write down one promise from Scripture that directly speaks to that fear. Then take a moment to pray that verse back to God, asking Him to make it alive in your heart today.

Day 7

He Is Strong When You Are Weak

Scripture:

"My grace is sufficient for you, for my power is made perfect in weakness." **2 Corinthians 12:9a**

Devotion:

You weren't meant to carry it all. You weren't built to handle every burden or hold everything together. That's God's job.

And the beautiful news? He doesn't expect strength from you; He offers it to you.

When you feel tired, worn out, or fragile, you are not failing; you are human. You're being invited to lean. God doesn't wait until you're strong to show up. He meets you in your weakness, and that's where His power shines the brightest.

Don't be afraid to come to Him depleted. He is your strength when yours runs out.

Prayer:

Lord, I bring You my weakness today. Instead of hiding it, I place it in Your hands. Be my strength where mine is gone, and let Your power shine through my dependence on You. Amen.

Reflection:

Where are you feeling weak at the moment? Let yourself name it honestly. Then ask God to be your strength in that exact place today.

Day 8

His Love Never Changes

Scripture:

"Give thanks to the Lord, for he is good; his love endures forever."
Psalm 107:1

Devotion:

In a world where love often feels fragile and dependent, measured by how much we achieve, how we look, or how well we behave, it is easy to grow weary and insecure. Human affection can fade, but God's love is different. His love is not swayed by mood, mistakes, or seasons. It is steady. Unchanging. Eternal.

You cannot out-sin it. You cannot outrun it. And you certainly don't have to perform to keep it. His love is a covenant, not a contract.

When everything around you shifts, friendships grow distant, emotions rise and fall, and circumstances shake your sense of security, God's love stands firm like an anchor in a storm. Fix your eyes on this truth, and fear will begin to lose its power.

Prayer:

Heavenly Father, thank You for the unchanging nature of Your love. On the days when I feel forgotten, unworthy, or unloved, remind me that nothing can separate me from the love You have poured out through Christ. Teach me to rest, not in my feelings, but in the certainty of Your everlasting affection. Amen.

Reflection:

Have there been moments when you doubted God's love for you, perhaps after a failure, a disappointment, or a season of silence? Write them down, and beside each one declare this truth: "God's love for me never changes; His love endures forever."

Day 9

He Sees the Big Picture

Scripture:

"As the heavens are higher than the earth, so are my ways higher than your ways and my thoughts than your thoughts." **Isaiah 55:9**

Devotion:

We often crave control. We want to know what's around the corner, to see how every detail of our lives will unfold, and to understand why certain things happen. But the life of faith calls us into something different; it calls us to rest in the hands of a God who sees the beginning, the middle, and the end all at once.

Time, emotions, or circumstances do not limit God's perspective. He sees the parts of the story you cannot see — the opportunities ahead, the lessons within the struggle, and the victory that is still in the making. While our view is often narrow and focused on "right now", His vision stretches far beyond the moment into eternity.

Think of it like a tapestry. From the underside, all you see are knots and tangled threads that look messy and confusing. But from above, the Weaver sees the design taking shape into something beautiful. In the same way, even when life feels unfair, uncertain, or incomplete, God is weaving your story into something purposeful and good.

You may not understand the "why" right now. But you can always trust the "Who". His character never changes. His love never fails. His plan never wavers.

Prayer:

Lord, when I can't trace Your plan, help me to trust Your heart. Teach me to rest in the truth that You see what I cannot. Remind me that my confusion is not a sign of Your absence but an opportunity for my faith to grow. May I surrender my questions into Your hands and find peace in knowing that Your ways are higher and wiser. Amen.

Reflection:

Where are you currently struggling to understand God's plan in your life? Write out your honest questions, and then speak truth over your heart: God sees the big picture. He is working all things together for my good.

Day 10

He Is Steady When Life Shifts

Scripture:

"We fix our eyes not on what is seen, but on what is unseen, since what is seen is temporary, but what is unseen is eternal." **2 Corinthians 4:18**

Devotion:

Life often feels like walking on unsteady ground. The headlines change daily, finances rise and fall, relationships stretch thin, and emotions swing like a pendulum. If we anchor our hearts to what we see, we'll constantly be pulled into fear, worry, and restlessness.

But God invites us to a higher focus. He calls us to lift our gaze above the noise, beyond the shifting shadows of this world, and fix our eyes on Him, the One who never changes.

When we choose to see with eyes of faith, we find that His presence steadies us, His promises hold us, and His goodness becomes our anchor. The storm may rage, but peace grows unshaken when it's rooted in the eternal.

Prayer:

Father, thank you for being steady, even when life feels unstable. Lift my eyes above the distractions and help me to fix them on what is eternal. Anchor my heart in Your presence so I can walk in peace today. Amen.

Reflection:

What has been distracting your focus lately? Name it honestly. Then ask God to help you lift your eyes to what is eternal.

Day 11

His Goodness Is Constant

Scripture:

"Surely your goodness and love will follow me all the days of my life…"
Psalm 23:6a

Devotion:

God's goodness is not conditional. It doesn't rise and fall with your emotions, and it isn't limited to seasons of success or celebration. His goodness follows you; steadily, faithfully, all the days of your life.

That means His goodness is present in moments of joy and in valleys of grief. It is there in seasons of clarity and in days of confusion. It surrounds you in times of calm, and it holds you steady in the middle of chaos.

Even when you cannot see it, His goodness is pursuing you. Even when the evidence seems hidden, it is there, woven into the ordinary details of your life, strengthening you in the difficult places.

You don't always need to feel it to believe it. You only need to trust it, and as you train your eyes to look for His goodness, you will begin to notice it everywhere.

Prayer:

Lord, thank You that Your goodness never leaves me. Even when I struggle to recognise it, I can rest in the truth that it is always with me, following me every day of my life. Open my eyes to see Your goodness in both the ordinary and the extraordinary today. Amen.

Reflection:

Take a moment to look back over this past week. Where did you see a glimpse of God's goodness, whether in a significant breakthrough or a small detail? Write it down as a reminder that His goodness is still chasing after you.

____

____

____

____

____

____

____

____

____

____

____

____

____

____

____

____

____

Day 12

His Mercy Meets You There

Scripture:

"Because of the Lord's great love, we are not consumed, for his compassions never fail. They are new every morning; great is your faithfulness." **Lamentations 3:22–23**

Devotion:

When we stumble, when anxiety grips our hearts, or when fear clouds our decisions, we often imagine God stepping back in disappointment. But the truth is just the opposite: His mercy leans in closer. His compassion is not repelled by our weakness; it is drawn to it.

You don't need to have everything figured out before His mercy reaches you. You don't need to feel strong before His strength carries you. Every morning, before you even take your first breath of the day, His mercies are already waiting; fresh, abundant, faithful, and overflowing.

Instead of replaying yesterday's failures, look up to His faithfulness today. His mercy is not just "enough" for you; it is more than enough. It covers, restores, and strengthens in ways you could never do on your own.

Prayer:

Father, thank You that Your mercies never expire and Your compassion never fails. When I feel crushed by regret, anxiety, or shame, remind me that You move toward me, not away. Help me let go of guilt and receive the freedom of Your love. Teach me to live this day rooted in Your mercy, walking in confidence because You are faithful. Amen.

Reflection:

What specific burden, guilt, fear, or shame do you need to release into God's hands today? Write it down, surrender it to Him, and receive His compassion as a fresh gift for this morning.

Day 13

He Is Your Peace

Scripture:

"The Lord gives strength to his people; the Lord blesses his people with peace." **Psalm 29:11**

Devotion:

True peace isn't the result of everything going right. It doesn't come from a life without problems, a calendar without interruptions, or a mind without questions. Peace is not the absence of struggle; it's the presence of God.

You can stand in the middle of uncertainty, with answers still hidden and storms still raging, and yet experience a stillness that doesn't make sense to the world. Why? Because God is not waiting for the storm to end before He shows up. He is present within it, holding you steady when everything else shakes.

When you shift your focus from the noise around you to the nearness of the One within you, peace begins to guard your heart. He doesn't shout above the chaos; He whispers calm into it. The world offers temporary relief, but Christ offers lasting peace — peace that carries you, strengthens you, and reminds you that you are never alone.

Prayer:

Prince of Peace, step into the chaos of my heart today. Where fear speaks loudly, let Your calm speak louder. Anchor me in Your presence and teach me to rest in the peace only You provide. Thank You for being near; not just when life is calm, but even when it feels uncertain. Amen.

Reflection:

What part of your life feels unsettled or overwhelming right now? Take a moment to invite God's peace into that space, and notice how His presence changes the way you carry it.

Day 14

He Brings Clarity

Scripture:

"Your word is a lamp for my feet, a light on my path." **Psalm 119:105**

Devotion:

Anxiety clouds our thinking. It fills our minds with "what ifs", worst-case scenarios, and overwhelming loops of fear. But God's Word cuts through the confusion. It lights the way.

You don't need to see the whole road ahead of you. You just need enough light for the next step. And when you fix your eyes on His truth, that's exactly what He gives you.

Focus on His Word today, not as a checklist, but as your compass. Let it be the voice that rises above the others, bringing clarity to your spirit.

Prayer:

Lord, thank You for the clarity Your Word brings. When my thoughts are tangled and my heart is restless, speak into the chaos. Shine Your light on the step before me, and teach me to walk with confidence, trusting that You are leading me every moment. Amen.

Reflection:

Where in your life does confusion feel heavy right now? Invite God to shine His light there, and ask Him to guide you one faithful step at a time.

Day 15

He Never Changes

Scripture:

"Jesus Christ is the same yesterday and today and forever." **Hebrews 13:8**

Devotion:

The world around us is in constant motion. Seasons shift, circumstances flip overnight, and our emotions often swing like a pendulum. In the middle of all this change, it's easy to feel unsettled or even lost. Yet for the believer, there is one steady anchor: the unchanging nature of Jesus Christ.

The same Lord who split the Red Sea, who touched lepers and made them whole, who spoke a word and stilled the storm, He is the very same today. His power has not weakened, His promises have not expired, and His love has not faded. He remains present in both your victories and your valleys, in moments of clarity as well as confusion, in your strength and even in your weakness.

When you choose to fix your eyes on Him, the One who is constant, unwavering, and forever faithful, you'll discover a peace that no shifting circumstance can take away. His unchanging nature becomes your sure foundation when everything else feels uncertain.

Prayer:

Unchanging and faithful God, thank You for being my steady foundation. When life feels unpredictable, remind me that You are the same yesterday, today, and forever. Anchor my heart in Your truth, and let Your unchanging love give rest and peace to my soul. Amen.

Reflection:

What aspect of God's character do you most need to cling to today: His faithfulness, His love, His power, or His wisdom? Write it down as a reminder that, while life shifts, God remains constant.

Day 16

Strength That Doesn't Come from You

Scripture:

"He gives strength to the weary and increases the power of the weak."
Isaiah 40:29

Devotion:

There are days when exhaustion takes over: mind, body, and heart. In those moments, weakness can feel like failure. But God never asked you to carry life in your own strength. He meets you in your frailty with His endless supply of power.

Real strength doesn't come from pushing harder, faking a smile, or pretending all is well. It comes from surrender; laying down what you can't handle and fixing your eyes on the One who never grows weary. His strength is steady when yours runs dry.

Feeling weak doesn't make you unworthy; it makes you ready. It's in your emptiness that God fills, in your limitation that He empowers. When you shift your focus from your inability to His ability, you'll discover fresh courage to take the next step.

Prayer:

Lord, I bring You my weakness today. I admit I cannot carry everything on my own. Thank you for exchanging my weariness for Your strength. Fill me with Your Spirit, steady my steps, and carry me where I cannot go by myself. Amen.

Reflection:

Where do you feel most drained at the moment? Invite God into that space, and trust His strength to lift and sustain you today.

Day 17

He Is Always Working

Scripture:

"And we know that in all things God works for the good of those who love him, who have been called according to his purpose." **Romans 8:28**

Devotion:

Life often brings seasons that feel heavy, confusing, and filled with unanswered questions. In those moments, it's easy to wonder if anything good can come out of the pain you're facing. Yet Scripture reminds us that God is never idle. Even when circumstances feel silent or hopeless, He is faithfully working behind the scenes.

Your emotions do not limit God's goodness. Your fears do not shake his plans. His purposes are not delayed by your pain. Like a master weaver, He threads redemption through every detail of your story; even the broken strands you wish weren't there.

Hold fast to this truth today: what looks like ashes to you can become beauty in His hands. Trust that the God who began a good work in you is still working, and He will bring it to completion.

Prayer:

Father, thank You for being at work in every season of my life, even when I cannot see Your hand. Teach me to trust Your timing and Your process. Remind me that You can turn sorrow into joy and brokenness into beauty. I place my story fully into Your hands. Amen.

Reflection:

Is there an area of your life where it feels challenging to notice God's hand at work? Take a moment to write a short prayer of trust. It can be as simple as: "Lord, I don't understand, but I choose to trust You." Leave space for Him to move in ways you cannot yet see.

Day 18

His Love Isn't Shaken

Scripture:

"Though the mountains be shaken and the hills be removed, yet my un-failing love for you will not be shaken…" **Isaiah 54:10**

Devotion:

Mountains may crumble. Hills may disappear. Life itself may shift beneath your feet. But one thing will never move: the unfailing love of God.

Your emotions may rise and fall. Your confidence may weaken. Fear may whisper, and doubt may roar. But the love of your heavenly Father remains steady, unwavering, and eternal.

He doesn't withhold His love in your anxious days. He doesn't distance Himself when you fail or stumble. His love is not fragile; it is an anchor, holding you secure no matter what storms rage around you or battles stir within you.

When your mind fills with self-criticism or the lies of unworthiness, take a holy pause. Breathe deeply, and remind your heart of this truth: You are chosen, cherished, and loved by God, not because of what you have done, but because of who He is.

Let this truth re-centre your soul today.

Prayer:

Father, thank You that Your love for me cannot be shaken or removed. When lies of fear and unworthiness creep in, silence them with Your voice of truth. Plant in me the unshakeable assurance that I am forever loved, held, and secure in You. Amen.

Reflection:

What lies or false labels have you been holding onto? Let God's unshakable love rewrite your story with His truth. Today, write a personal affirmation beginning with: "God loves me, and His love never wavers…"

Day 19

In the Middle of the Storm

Scripture:

"Then they cried out to the Lord in their trouble, and he brought them out of their distress. He stilled the storm to a whisper; the waves of the sea were hushed." **Psalm 107:28–29**

Devotion:

Most of us believe peace will come after the storm is over, when the waves finally settle and the skies clear. However, the truth is, God doesn't wait for calm seas to appear. He is already present, steady, and near, right in the chaos.

The same God who once commanded the wind and waves to be still is the One who can quiet the noise inside your own soul. He sees the fear you try to hide, the questions you carry, and the exhaustion you feel. He is not far off, watching from the shore. He is in the boat with you.

So when everything around you feels unsettled, resist the urge to stare at the storm. Instead, lift your eyes to the One who holds authority over it. His presence doesn't just promise peace later; it provides peace now.

Prayer:

Jesus, thank You for meeting me in the middle of my storm. Speak calmly over my anxious heart and remind me that even here, I am not abandoned. Let Your voice rise above the waves, and whisper peace to my spirit as only You can. Amen.

Reflection:

What "storm" are you facing in this season of life? Close your eyes and imagine Jesus sitting with you in the very centre of it. What do you hear Him saying to you right now? Write it down.

Day 20

Truth That Breaks the Lie

Scripture:

"Then you will know the truth, and the truth will set you free." **John 8:32**

Devotion:

Anxiety thrives on lies. It whispers, "You're not safe." "You're not enough." "Things will never change." These thoughts echo like a broken record until they feel true. The enemy shouts them often, hoping repetition will convince your heart.

But truth speaks louder than lies, even when it comes in a gentle whisper. God's word carries unshakeable authority. His truth does not always immediately erase the storm, but it anchors you in the midst of it. Freedom comes not from the absence of struggle, but from seeing your circumstances through the lens of what God has already spoken.

God's truth sets you free, not because your circumstances change immediately, but because it changes how you see them. When you fix your mind on what is real, eternal, and unchanging, the lies begin to lose their grip.

Fix your eyes on what is eternal, not temporary. When you root yourself in what God says —unchanging, living, and powerful —the grip of fear begins to weaken. Lies lose their strength when confronted with the light of truth.

Prayer:

Lord, thank You that Your Word is life and freedom. When fear shouts, let Your truth rise louder in my heart. Teach me to cling to what You say about me and drown out every voice of doubt. Set me free today by the power of Your truth. Amen.

Reflection:

What anxious thought has been echoing in your mind? Find a scripture that directly speaks against it, write it down, and place it where you'll see it often today. Let God's Word answer the lie every time it resurfaces.

Day 21

Grace for Every Misstep

Scripture:

"My grace is sufficient for you, for my power is made perfect in weakness." **2 Corinthians 12:9**

Devotion:

You won't always get it right. Some days, fear will creep in and seem louder than faith. Other times, your thoughts may spiral so quickly that prayer feels out of reach. There will be moments you forget to pause, to breathe, or to lean into God's presence.

And yet, right there, in the middle of your mess, grace shows up.

God's love has never been tied to your flawless performance. His grace is not a pay cheque you work for; it's a gift that flows freely, fully, and endlessly. It meets you in your weakness, steadies you in your stumbles, and whispers, "You are still Mine."

So, when you fall short, resist the urge to collapse into shame. Instead, lift your eyes to the One whose grace covers every misstep. Let His mercy quiet your doubts, restore your confidence, and remind you that you are not defined by failure, but by His unfailing love. You are still learning, still held, still chosen.

Prayer:

Gracious Father, thank You for a love that doesn't measure me by my perfection. When I stumble, wrap me in Your grace and steady my steps. Teach me to see my weakness as a place for Your strength to shine. Remind me daily that I am Yours, still loved, and still growing in Your hands. Amen.

Reflection:

Where do you need God's grace most today? Write a gentle sentence to yourself as though the Lord is speaking directly to you, offering truth, reassurance, and hope.

Day 22

When Waiting Feels Heavy

Scripture:

"I remain confident of this: I will see the goodness of the Lord in the land of the living. Wait for the Lord; be strong and take heart and wait for the Lord." **Psalm 27:13–14**

Devotion:

Waiting is never easy. The longer the silence, the louder anxiety seems to grow. Our hearts begin to ask, 'Has God forgotten me?' Yet waiting is not the absence of God's presence; it is often the stage where He does His deepest, unseen work.

The real question is not 'Is God working?' but rather 'Am I willing to notice Him in the process, not just in the outcome?'

In God's hands, waiting is not wasted time. What feels like standing still is actually sacred ground — an invitation to trust, to rest, and to open our eyes to the subtle glimpses of His goodness. Sometimes the breakthrough comes later, but the blessing of His presence is available even now.

Prayer:

Lord, waiting feels heavy, and my heart often wrestles with uncertainty. But today I choose to place my hope in You. Strengthen me when I grow weary, give me courage when fear rises, and train my eyes to see Your goodness even before the answer arrives. Amen.

Reflection:

What are you waiting on God for in this season? Write a short prayer of trust, honest and real, even if your heart still feels uncertain.

Day 23

Anchored in Overwhelm

Scripture:

"You will keep in perfect peace those whose minds are steadfast, because they trust in you." **Isaiah 26:3**

Devotion:

Life has a way of piling up: one unexpected phone call, a deadline that feels impossible, or emotions that rise like a sudden storm. Overwhelm often comes without warning, leaving us feeling powerless, frantic, or tempted to run. But true peace is never found in escaping or numbing ourselves; it is discovered in the One who holds all things steady.

God invites us to anchor our hearts and minds in Him. He does not panic. He does not get swept away by the tide of our troubles. While everything around us may shift, His character remains unchanging, and His promises unshakeable. When our minds stay fixed on His truth, His peace guards us, even in the very centre of the chaos.

Your security is not found in your ability to hold it all together. Your anchor is not your strength; it is His faithfulness. And when the waves rise, His anchor holds firm.

Prayer:

Father, when life feels overwhelming and the weight of it presses in, remind me that You are my anchor. Steady my thoughts on Your truth, calm my racing heart, and keep me grounded in the peace only You can give. Hold me secure today. Amen.

Reflection:

Think of a time you felt overwhelmed, but God's peace carried you through. Write down a verse, prayer, or truth that helped you stay anchored. Keep it somewhere you can return to when the waves rise again.

____

____

____

____

____

Day 24

Strength for Today

Scripture:

"As your days, so shall your strength be." **Deuteronomy 33:25**

Devotion:

Sometimes our minds run ahead to tomorrow, stacking up fears and "what ifs" until today feels impossible to bear. But anxiety often begins not in the future; it starts in the present, when the weight of even this moment feels heavy.

God, however, doesn't ask you to carry tomorrow's burdens today. He promises strength for the exact day you are living right now. Just as He fed Israel with manna in the wilderness—fresh, daily bread that could not be stored up—He offers grace in real time. Yesterday's strength won't sustain you today, and tomorrow's hasn't arrived yet. But today's strength? It is here, poured out, enough for the path you are walking.

Being weary is not weakness. It is proof that you are human. And the beauty of being human is that we were never meant to be self-sufficient. Our limits are the very places where God meets us. His word reminds us: "My grace is sufficient for you, for My power is made perfect in weakness." (2 Corinthians 12:9).

So take a breath. Whisper a prayer. Lean into the truth that the God who carried you through yesterday is already standing in today with fresh mercy and strength. You don't have to run ahead. You don't have to figure it all out. You only need to walk with Him in this moment.

Prayer:

Lord, thank You for meeting me here, in this exact moment. Thank You that I don't need to borrow tomorrow's strength, because You give me enough for today. Teach me to rest in Your sufficiency and trust that when tomorrow comes, You'll be there too, with new mercies waiting. Amen.

Reflection:

Where are you tempted to borrow worries from tomorrow? Write down one specific area where you feel weak today, and then invite God's strength into it.

Day 25

Keep Looking Up

Scripture:

"I lift my eyes to the mountains — where does my help come from? My help comes from the Lord, the Maker of heaven and earth." **Psalm 121:1–2**

Devotion:

When life presses in, fear always tries to drag our gaze downward, toward problems, pain, and uncertainty. But Scripture gently redirects us: Look up.

True help doesn't come from our own strength, quick fixes, or perfectly arranged circumstances. It flows from the unchanging character of the Lord, the Maker of the heavens, the One who holds the world in place and holds your heart in His hands.

Every upward glance toward Him re-centres your focus. Each time you choose to lift your eyes in faith, you remind your soul: I am not alone. I am not without help. I am entirely held by the One who never fails.

Prayer:

Lord, when my heart is heavy and my eyes want to fall on the problem, lift my gaze to You. Thank You for being my Helper, my Strength, and my steady Hope. Keep my eyes fixed upward, today and every day. Amen.

Reflection:

What situations have been stealing your focus and weighing you down? Write them out, then surrender them to God in prayer. As you do, thank Him for being your ever-present help and ask Him to lift your eyes to His promises.

Day 26

His Presence Is Enough

Scripture:

"My Presence will go with you, and I will give you rest." **Exodus 33:14**

Devotion:

We often believe peace will come once the problem is solved, the answer is clear, or the weight is finally lifted. But God's Word reminds us of a greater truth: peace is not found in the absence of trouble, but in the presence of God Himself.

Moses understood this when he pleaded, "If Your Presence does not go with us, do not send us up from here" (Exodus 33:15). He knew that no victory, no promised land, no blessing would matter without God walking beside him.

God may not always remove the challenge before you, but He promises something far better, His nearness. When you shift your gaze from the size of your burden to the greatness of His presence, your weary soul finds rest. His presence doesn't just comfort; it carries, sustains, and satisfies. Truly, His presence is enough.

Prayer:

Lord, thank You that I never walk alone. When I feel restless, remind me that true peace is found in You, not in my circumstances. Teach me to rest in Your presence today and trust that You are more than enough for every need I face. Be my peace, my strength, and my rest. Amen.

Reflection:

What burden feels heaviest today? Write it down, picture yourself laying it at the feet of Jesus, and ask Him to replace your restlessness with His peace.

Day 27

His Word Holds Steady

Scripture:

"The grass withers and the flowers fall, but the word of our God endures forever." **Isaiah 40:8**

Devotion:

Seasons shift. Circumstances change. Feelings rise and fall like the tide. Yet the Word of God stands unshaken. What He has spoken remains, firm and enduring, when everything else proves temporary.

When your heart feels unsettled, return to Scripture. Let His promises remind you of what is sure, what is lasting, and what cannot fail. His word is the anchor that steadies your soul in every storm.

Prayer:

Faithful Father, thank You that Your Word never changes. Root me deeply in Your truth and keep my heart steady when life feels uncertain. Let Your promises be the solid ground I walk on today. Amen.

Reflection:

Think back to a difficult season in your life. What verse sustained you during that time? Write it down again today, and let it be a fresh reminder that His Word endures through every change.

Day 28

He Holds Your Future

Scripture:

"For I know the plans I have for you," declares the Lord, "plans to prosper you and not to harm you, plans to give you hope and a future." **Jeremiah 29:11**

Devotion:

Anxiety often grows loud when our minds wander into tomorrow. What if things go wrong? What if the unknown is too heavy to carry? But you don't have to live in fear; your future is not fragile in God's hands.

He sees every detail you cannot, and His plans are always shaped by hope, not harm. Trust the One who has already gone before you. The same God who holds today will hold tomorrow, too.

Prayer:

Lord, thank You that my future is secure in Your care. Silence the noise of fear in my mind and replace it with confidence in Your good plans. Teach me to rest in the hope You provide. Amen.

Reflection:

What specific worries about tomorrow have been weighing on your heart? Write them down one by one, and prayerfully surrender each into God›s hands.

Day 29

His Joy Is Your Strength

Scripture:

"Do not grieve, for the joy of the Lord is your strength." Nehemiah 8:10b

Devotion:

There are seasons when the weight of life presses hard, leaving us drained and weary. In those moments, joy may feel distant, like something we must strive to find. However, the truth is that joy is not something we create on our own; it is a gift freely given by God. His joy flows from His presence, not from our circumstances.

The joy of the Lord becomes an anchor when your strength is slipping away. It lifts your heart when discouragement whispers that you cannot keep going. It does not deny sorrow or pretend pain does not exist, but it reminds you that sorrow does not have the final word. In Christ, there is always hope.

When you lean into His joy, you begin to see even the smallest blessings, such as sunlight through a window, laughter with a friend, or a verse that speaks right on time, as reminders of His sustaining love. Each glimpse of joy becomes a spark of strength, carrying you through what once felt impossible.

Prayer:

Father, I thank You that Your joy is more than a feeling; it is my strength and my steady foundation. On the days when I am weak and worn out, remind me that Your joy is already within me because You are with me. Help me recognise the little moments of pleasure You send each day and let them renew my heart, refresh my spirit, and keep me walking in hope. In Jesus' name, Amen.

Reflection:

Think back over today: where did you glimpse God's joy, perhaps in creation, a kind word, or a quiet moment of peace? Write it down, and consider how that moment can serve as a reminder that His joy is carrying you, even now.

Day 30

Closing Reflection –
Eyes Fixed on Eternity

Scripture:

"Since then, you have been raised with Christ, set your hearts on things above, where Christ is…" **Colossians 3:1**

Devotion:

It's so easy for our gaze to settle on what is right in front of us: the anxieties, disappointments, and pressures of daily life. The temporary shouts loudly, while the eternal often whispers. Yet Paul's reminder in Colossians is clear: we are no longer bound to the temporary. We have been raised with Christ, and our eyes are fixed on Him.

When we shift our focus heavenward, the weight of today begins to feel lighter. Worries no longer define us, because our hope is anchored in what cannot be shaken. Fixing our hearts on eternity does not erase challenges, but it reframes them. The troubles of today are momentary compared to the glory of forever with Christ (2 Corinthians 4:17).

Living with eternity in view brings courage when fear rises, endurance when trials persist, and peace when uncertainty looms. Christ's victory guarantees our hope, and His presence secures our peace.

Prayer:

Lord, realign my heart today. Teach me to look beyond what is passing and to fix my eyes on what is eternal. Anchor my hope in Christ alone, and let the reality of eternity shape how I live, think, and love today. May Your presence guide my focus and guard my peace. Amen.

Reflection:

What concern has consumed your attention recently? Write it down, then place it beside the eternal promises of God. How does viewing it through the lens of eternity change the weight it holds in your heart?

CONCLUSION
Keep Lifting Your Eyes

Dear Friend,

You've just completed 30 intentional days of fixing your gaze on the One who never shifts, never fails, and never changes. Every verse you held close, every whispered prayer, every anxious thought you surrendered, none of it was wasted. Each small step you've taken is part of God's transforming work, planting seeds of truth that will continue to grow in you.

Fixing your eyes on Him doesn't erase the presence of fear or silence every anxious thought forever. But it does mean that fear no longer gets the final say. You are learning a new way of living; one where peace has room to breathe, truth anchors your soul, and God's steady presence carries you when life feels shaky and uncertain.

So don't stop now. Keep showing up with a heart that says yes to Him. Keep lifting your eyes when the weight of life tries to drag them down. Keep reminding yourself of who God is, even when circumstances shout a different story. Each time you choose Him over fear, your mind is being renewed, and little by little, peace takes deeper root, one faithful thought at a time.

I am deeply proud of you for walking through this journey. And I believe with confidence that as you continue to hold fast to God's unchanging character, His peace will not only guard your heart but will overflow into your life in ways far greater than you can imagine.

With love and encouragement,

Robin

About The Author

Robin Kite is a Christian writer, speaker, and former educator with a heart for helping women rediscover peace, clarity, and God-given purpose. What began as a quiet practice of journaling and prayer during her own faith journey blossomed into a ministry of encouragement that now reaches countless women through devotionals and Scripture-based colouring books.

Her works, including the Amazon bestseller A 30-Day Devotional for Women: Renew Your Faith, Purpose, and Self-Discovery, invite readers to find comfort in chaos, hope in waiting seasons, and renewed strength when life feels overwhelming.

Together with her husband, Robin also leads a nonprofit ministry established in memory of their daughter, offering practical support and spiritual encouragement to children and families in need within their community.

Whether through writing or ministry, Robin's mission remains clear: to remind women that their healing is valuable, their purpose is God-designed, and their story is still being beautifully written.

Thank You

Thank you for joining me in 'The 30-Day Devotional for Women, Connect Deeper With God To Move From Anxiety and Fear To Faith, Strength, Love and Lasting Peace.' I am deeply honored that you chose to walk through these 30 days, setting aside time to pause, reflect, and draw nearer to God in the midst of life's changes.

My prayer is that these devotionals have filled your heart with encouragement, renewed your strength, and given you a peace that lasts beyond these pages. May the truths of God's word continue to guide and steady you in every season.

If this devotional has been meaningful to you, I'd love it if you left a quick Amazon review. Your feedback not only helps me grow as a writer but also makes it easier for others to discover the encouragement within these pages.

From my heart to yours, thank you for allowing me to be part of your journey of faith.

With gratitude,

Robin

"Fixing our eyes on Jesus, the pioneer and perfecter of faith." — Hebrews 12:2

BONUS #2:

Peace Habit Starter Kit

■ **Your Free Gift**

If the Peace Plan helps you find calm in the moment, imagine having a step-by-step system that trains your mind and heart to live in that peace every single day. That's exactly what the Peace Habit Starter Kit is designed for.

■ **Get instant access here:**

■ Scan the QR code below to grab your copy instantly:

Made with Flodesk

■ **Inside the Kit, You'll Discover:**

■ **AM & PM Peace Cards** — quick 2–5 minute daily reset routines

■ **30-Day Peace Checklist** — stay consistent and encouraged

■ **Habit Tracker** — build your "peace streak" one day at a time

■ **Trigger–Action–Reward (TAR) Plan** — make peace automatic

■ **Accountability Tools** — simple prompts to help you stay on track

■ Together, **Bonus #1: The Peace Plan** and **Bonus #2: The Peace Habit Starter Kit** give you both the **quick reset** and the **long-term rhythm** for building a life of peace.